GROWING INTO THE IMAGE OF CHRIST

A Biblical Perspective On Spiritual Maturity

Wale Babatunde

Christian Heritage Publication
An Imprint of
Great Commission Incorporation
25-27 Ruby Street
Off Old Kent Road
London
SE15 1LR
United Kingdom

Copyright © Wale Babatunde 2017-03-21
The moral right of the author has been asserted in accordance with the Copyright Designs and Patent Act 1988
All rights reserved. No part of this publication may be reproduced, stored in a retrieval system, or transmitted in any form or by any means, electronic, mechanical, photocopying or otherwise, without the prior written consent of the publisher; short extracts may be used for review purposes.
Scripture Quotations are taken from:
King James Bible. © Crown Copyright
Used by permission. All rights reserved
ISBN: 978-0-9570933-5-5
Cover design: SpiffingCovers Ltd
Book Transformation Work (Copy Editing & Proofreading) – Mrs. Nana Fosua Babatunde
Printed and bound in the UK by SpiffingCovers Ltd

Contents

DEDICATION	5
FOREWORD	7
INTRODUCTION	9
CHAPTER 1 - SALVATION – MAN'S GREATEST NEED	11
CHAPTER 2 - THE BELIEVER'S ULTIMATE DESTINY	13
CHAPTER 3 - THE PROCESS OF SPIRITUAL GROWTH	17
CHAPTER 4 - SPIRITUAL MATURITY AND INHERITANCE	25
CHAPTER 5 - SIGNS OF SPIRITUAL MATURITY	29
CHAPTER 6 - CONSEQUENCES OF SPIRITUAL STAGNATION	37
CHAPTER 7 - WHY THE DOMA GIFTS?	45
CHAPTER 8 - WHAT ON EARTH ARE WE FEEDING THE CHURCH?	49
CHAPTER 9 - SPIRITUAL MATURITY AND ADVERSITY	55
CHAPTER 10 - ISRAEL SPEAKS TO US TODAY!	59
CHAPTER 11 - LIKE FATHER, LIKE SON	63
SPECIAL INVITATION	67
OTHER TITLES FROM THE SAME AUTHOR	69
CONTACT DETAILS	71

Dedication

I dedicate this book to our Lord and Saviour, Jesus Christ, for giving me what I consider the greatest privilege in my life to serve in the Kingdom of God. He has been faithful all through the years and I am ever so grateful. Jesus, I love you; Jesus, I thank you; Jesus, I bless you for journeying with me all these years.

Foreword

At the 'New Birth' experience in Christ, the Lord gave us His Holy Spirit for the Salvation of our Souls. By this, every Believer becomes a New Creation in Christ Jesus. Not only did The Lord give us His Holy Spirit, but also the Gifts of Apostles, Prophets, Evangelists, Pastors and Teachers for our journey of salvation.

These Gifts are to equip and edify us with the goal of bringing the Church to the knowledge of the Son of God (the Perfect Man) so that with this knowledge, we, the Saints, will be able to reflect the Image of Christ and no other image aimed at satisfying the flesh.

In this book, Pastor Wale Babatunde has been able to explain in a simple way, the different stages of the Believer's growth into the Image of Christ, what may hinder this growth, and how we must repent, gaining the Salvation of our Souls which our Lord Jesus Christ is coming back for.

This book contains an end time message from the

Lord Jesus to prepare us for His coming as Wise Virgins. The main preoccupation of every Believer should be to be conformed to the Image of Christ.

I would recommend this book to all Christians and also for use in House Churches, Bible Study Groups and Christian Foundational Classes in the Church.

Dapo Benzoe
National Overseer
World Harvest Christian Centre
The United Kingdom.

Introduction

Our acceptance of Christ's Gift of Salvation is the Greatest privilege we can ever have in life. We become New Creations and are joined to the Body of Christ. As physical as our lives may be here on earth, we have a Spiritual Mandate of working out our salvation with Jesus Christ as the focal point of reference.

Everything we do as Believers must, therefore, be what our Risen Lord will have us doing. Sad to say, we live in the end times, where the pursuit of many is self-centred and not Christ-centred. As a result, Believers are failing to grow spiritually into the Image of Christ. How can we justify our drive to excel and progress in all physical spheres of life but can't boast of exerting that same energy in the things of the Spirit?

At the end of the day, your life will count as well-lived if only it was aimed at being more like Jesus and maturing in the Holy Faith. Refrain from being a Child in the Kingdom and mature into a Father. Maturity in

God's Kingdom is not by age but by Grace. I believe with all of my heart that God is seeking a generation that will rise up and invest earnestly in pursuing spiritual matters that will count for eternity.

I am grateful to God for giving me this Revelation to share with you and I will entreat you to make a decision today to Grow Into the Image of Christ. With the help of the Holy Spirit, your life will be transformed and your ways shall please the LORD.

CHAPTER 1
SALVATION – MAN'S GREATEST NEED

Every human being has certain basic needs requisite for them to function or live properly, and are categorised as physical, emotional, psychological, and Spiritual needs. As far as I am concerned, man's greatest need is to be reconciled to his Maker. As a result, we are to find peace with God after we have received the free offer of Salvation through the finished work on the Cross.

There is a void in the heart of every man that we often try to find substitutes like pleasures, relationships, education and even money, to fill. Many try religion, yet this peace eludes them. There is only one way to God, and this is through the atoning work of Jesus Christ. The Scriptures make it abundantly clear that God wants everyone to be saved and to make heaven.

"The Lord is not slack concerning his promise, as

some men count slackness; but is longsuffering to us-ward, not willing that any should perish, but that all should come to repentance."

– 2 Peter 3:9 (KJV).

"For this is good and acceptable in the sight of God our Saviour; Who will have all men to be saved, and to come unto the knowledge of the truth."

– 1 Timothy 2:3-4 (KJV).

It does not matter how many worldly assets, goods and treasures one possesses as they cannot compare to the salvation of one's soul. Therefore, The Scriptures declare:

"For what is a man profited, if he shall gain the whole world, and lose his own soul? or what shall a man give in exchange for his soul?"

– Matthew 16:26 (KJV).

Nothing in this world can be compared to the Salvation of our souls. The whole world put together is not as valuable as the soul of an individual. This is the premium that God and the Bible place on the soul of an individual. It cost God the life of His **ONLY** Son – Jesus Christ. This is why the one thread that runs through the whole of the Bible from Genesis to Revelation is the story of how God tries to bring back 'fallen man' from Adam's loins unto Himself.

Chapter 2

THE BELIEVER'S ULTIMATE DESTINY

"For whom he did foreknow, he also did predestinate to be conformed to the image of his Son, that he might be the firstborn among many brethren."

– Romans 8:29 (KJV).

After salvation, God has an ultimate destiny for every bonafide child of His, which is, to be conformed to the Image of His Son – Jesus Christ. Jesus came into this world, not just to die in our place and reveal the Father's will to us, but came to show us what it means to be a Son of God.

Jesus is also the firstborn among many brethren. I am a Child of God; you are also a Child of God. However, Jesus came to earth to show us by example, through His life – deeds, words and character, how to live as a Son of God. This is why Paul declared that we have been predestined to be conformed to the Image of God's Son.

This teaching is very much lacking in the Church today. For so many years, I never realised how important this was to God. Can you imagine the consequence of omitting this important truth in our teaching and nurturing in the Body of Christ? For so long, I thought that God was primarily interested in saving me from the power and penalty of sin, guaranteeing me a place in heaven, and in return, I was to serve and love Him with all of my heart. Sadly, I was totally wrong. God desires Sons and Daughters that will reflect the Image of His Son, Jesus Christ.

YOUR ULTIMATE DESTINY

Over the last few decades, there has been a lot of emphasis on Believers fulfilling their destinies. By the Grace of God, I must have preached a lot of messages on this topic, and written a few books. The mistake that I and many Believers, and I dare say, Ministers of the Gospel make is that, when we speak about fulfilling destiny, we refer to accomplishing feats such as becoming a lawyer, medical doctor, sportsman or woman, or even a Minister of the Gospel. However, these can never be our ultimate destiny in life. Our ultimate and authentic destiny is to become like Jesus. It is possible to become an athlete, musician, lawyer or medical doctor, and yet never look like the Son of God.

THE SECOND TRAVAIL

The Bible speaks of the second travail that many Believers may not be familiar with. Paul alludes to this in his Epistle to the Galatians, when he addressed his spiritual children and his role in their spiritual formation.

"My little children, of whom I travail in birth again until Christ be formed in you."
- Galatians 4:19 (KJV).

Notice Paul's choice of words: 'travail in birth again'. Who travails, and when? By natural laws, women who go into labour are the ones that travail. Travailing always precedes childbirth and it is accompanied by excruciating pain. This is the first travail which brings to birth every sinner. For anyone to have found Christ, someone somewhere must have paid the price in travail.

However, there is a second travail that Pastors, Spiritual mentors, Ministers of the DOMA Gifts and all those who have spiritual oversight have to go through in order to bring about the formation of Christ in the lives of Believers. This is what Paul was doing with the Saints in Galatia.

The fact that a woman conceives a baby does not guarantee the full development of the foetus. Some result in miscarriages, stillbirths or under-developed babies. In the same vein, being a Believer does not necessarily mean that Christ is fully formed in a person.

The unfortunate thing today is that most Believers never transition from being a Child of God (born again Believer) to a Son of God (being conformed into His Image).

CHAPTER 3
THE PROCESS OF SPIRITUAL GROWTH

Without controversy, spiritual growth is the key or pathway to being conformed to the Image of Christ. Spiritual growth itself doesn't occur in an instant - it is a process. Just as a baby has to go through different stages of development into adulthood, so also does a Christian have to pass through different phases of spiritual development.

In any army barracks, everyone is collectively referred to as a soldier, however, they are set apart by ranks. There are majors, captains, colonels, lieutenants, and generals, to mention these few. Even among the Generals, there are different levels – five, four, three, two, and one star respectively.

In this chapter, I am going to attempt to highlight the various stages of spiritual formation. The purpose will be to challenge the reader not to be complacent with their spiritual growth but to aspire to reach the pinnacle, as far as their spiritual formation is concerned.

1. NEWBORN BABES (Brephos - Greek)
"As newborn babes, desire the sincere milk of the word, that ye may grow thereby."

- 1 Peter 2:2 (KJV).

This is the first stage of spiritual development. Newborn babes or newborn infants – this speaks of a child or babe who has just been freshly delivered. An example is a day, week or month old baby.

2. BABES (Nepios - Greek)
"And I, brethren, could not speak unto you as unto spiritual, but as unto carnal, even as unto babes in Christ"

- 1 Corinthians 3:1 (KJV).

The Greek word for babes here is Nepios referring to an infant – a minor. This speaks of simple-minded and immature Christians. This was the state of the Corinthian Church, even though they were the most gifted in the New Testament. We can conclude from this book that, the operation of spiritual gifts is no guarantee of Spiritual Maturity. This was the spiritual state of the recipients of the Epistles to the Hebrews; they suffered from a stagnant spiritual growth.

"Of whom we have many things to say, and hard to be uttered, seeing ye are dull of hearing. For when for the time ye ought to be teachers, ye have need that one teach you again which be the first principles of the oracles of God; and are become such as have need of milk, and not of strong meat. For every one that useth milk is unskilful in the word of righteousness: for he is a babe."

– Hebrews 5:11-13 (KJV).

Apart from the two categorizations above of spiritual formation, I believe Apostle John, the writer of the Epistle of John, has further enlightened us on this subject matter. In 1 John 2:12-14, he highlighted three levels of spiritual formation:

"I write unto you, little children, because your sins are forgiven you for his name's sake. I write unto you, fathers, because ye have known him that is from the beginning. I write unto you, young men, because ye have overcome the wicked one. I write unto you, little children, because ye have known the Father. I have written unto you, fathers, because ye have known him that is from the beginning. I have written unto you, young men, because ye are strong, and the word of God abideth in you, and ye have overcome the wicked one."

– 1 John 2:12-14 (KJV).

3. LITTLE CHILDREN (Teknion - Greek) – A Christian convert

Notice what the Apostle says about this category of Christians? Their sins have been forgiven, and now they have known the Father. Forgiveness of sins is what qualifies one to have a Relationship with God.

4. YOUNG MEN (Neaniskos - Greek)

In Greek terminology, this category refers to a youth or a young man that is under the age of forty. In spiritual terms, notice with me characteristics of the young men:

a. They have overcome the wicked one.
b. They are strong; "and the word of God abideth in you, and ye have overcome the wicked one."

The young men are strong because of the influence of the Word of God. These men give the Word of God a central place in their lives. They have come to understand that man does not live by bread alone, but by every Word that proceeds out of the mouth of God. They are very skilful in the Word of Righteousness.

Just like their Saviour, they have overcome the enemy by what is written.

"And they overcame him by the blood of the

Lamb, and by the word of their testimony..."
*– **Revelations 12:11 (KJV)**.*

Can you identify people in your circle of influence who belong to this stage in their spiritual formation?

5. FATHERS (Pater - Greek) – Parent
The key word about fathers in this passage is "KNOWN".

"... ye have known him that is from the beginning..."(Verse 13, 14).

What truth is the Apostle trying to convey about the father, in relation to spiritual growth?
- INTIMACY!

Fathers have an intimate relationship with God. They have progressed from not just knowing the Word of God, like many people do today, to knowing the GOD of the Word. Most of us use products and services manufactured by certain individuals, but only a few have the privilege of meeting and knowing intimately the brains behind these products. Many of us today have Microsoft computers in our homes, yet only a few have met the man behind this invention – Bill Gates. Most Christians today simply have a mental assent of

God. Like the children of Israel, we only know the Acts of God, but not His ways.

Have you noticed that the key to fruitfulness and reproduction is intimacy? To be fruitful, a man must be intimate with a woman; in the same vein, if we are going to be fruitful and bring forth fruits that will abide, we must be intimate with God. No wonder Paul's passion/drive was to know Christ more than anything else!

> *"That I may know him, and the power of his resurrection, and the fellowship of his sufferings, being made conformable unto his death."*
> **– Philippians 3:10 (KJV).**

Again, *"... for I know whom I have believed, and am persuaded that he is able to keep that which I have committed unto him against that day."*
– 2 Timothy 1:12b (KJV).

Fathers take responsibility. They are responsible for lives; they provide for their dependants; they are the priests, prophets, protectors, providers and potentates of their homes.

Spiritual fatherhood has little to do with age. You can be seventy or eighty years old, and yet a babe in Christ. I am a Spiritual Father to many who are old enough to be my biological father. When you meet someone, who is a true Spiritual Father in every sense of the word, they are more interested in deepening their knowledge or relationship with Christ. They are not easily carried away by all the modern day spiritual razzmatazz! Ministerial responsibilities or accomplishments do not come before one's intimate Relationship with God as far as true spiritual fathers are concerned.

If it is indeed true that Christians have to go through different stages of spiritual development or formation, is it not then reasonable to think that Ministers and Ministries should set out as part of their goals, programmes, teachings and curriculum geared towards spiritual formation and development?

CHAPTER 4
SPIRITUAL MATURITY AND INHERITANCE

The level of your Spiritual Maturity is a critical factor in determining your position, authority and responsibility in the Kingdom of God.

In the British or American army, for example, all those who have attained the ranking of a General, must have been experienced and fully matured. In the same vein, God will only commit real treasures (by this, I am not speaking about money or worldly materials) into the hands of Spiritually Matured Saints, who have been processed in Heaven's school.

The Scriptures teach that as Believers, 'all things are ours' as we are heirs and joint-heirs with Christ thus having access to everything that belongs to God. However, God will often withhold these things from spiritually immature children until such a time that they are spiritually mature. This is the reason why Paul referenced that even though a Believer might be the heir apparent, they are treated as the servant.

> *"Now I say,* That *the heir, as long as he is a child, differeth nothing from a servant, though he be lord of all."*
> **– Galatians 4:1 (KJV).**

The question is – who commits their riches or inheritance into the hands of servants or children? Most parents, when writing their will, would often stipulate an adult age for their estate to be handed over to their wards, should they die.

I love my teenage son a lot, and I would love to give or bless him with some of my worldly goods, but I can't do that at the moment because his maturity is not commensurate to the things I would love to give him. What then can I do? Wait until such a time I perceive that he has become mature enough to handle such inheritance, and it will not damage or destroy him.

CHURCH LEADERSHIP
I believe it is for the same reason that Paul the Apostle when writing about the Spiritual qualifications of a would-be Bishop or Spiritual Leader, stated categorically that the person must not be a novice or a recent convert.

> *"Not a novice, lest being lifted up with pride he fall into the condemnation of the devil."*
> **– 1 Timothy 3:6 (KJV).**

WHY THE DELAY?

Quite often, we face one form of delay or the other. For some, it is a delay in childbirth; for others, it is a delay in relationships, marriage, education or career! The list is endless. There are different reasons why people experience delays, they include – sin, ignorance, character flaws and laziness, amongst many others.

I have come to discover, however, that one of the key reasons why Christians experience delay is because they have refused to grow spiritually. God will often withhold certain blessings from His children because to bless them will jeopardise their spiritual well-being. I have often said that prosperity without Spirituality will end up being a casualty!

CHAPTER 5
SIGNS OF SPIRITUAL MATURITY

Is it possible for a Believer to recognise when they or others are maturing in Christ? Are there some indicators to look out for as possible signs that I am growing in Christ?

Before we highlight a few points, I believe it is needful to mention some things that do not constitute or mean that a person is maturing in the Christian faith.

1. REGULAR CHURCH ATTENDANCE

Often, when people want to justify their spirituality, they point to the fact that they attend Church services regularly. While this is commendable and often a reflection of a desire for spiritual things, it is however not a guarantee that you are maturing spiritually. Many go for fellowship three times or even more every week, yet it is simply a "religious" observance – they don't know Jesus Christ as their Lord and Personal Saviour. People attend fellowships for different principal reasons, including going to look for a Christian spouse or partner, business contacts or prosperity.

2. OBSERVANCE OF SPIRITUAL DISCIPLINES

All religions observe different types of spiritual disciplines. They include prayer, fasting, meditation and alms-giving, just to mention a few. Cornelius, the Centurion, was described as a devout man; one that feared God with all his house and gave much alms to the needy. He was also a man that prayed and fasted often, yet he had no living Relationship with God until Peter preached The Gospel to Him (Acts 10:1-4).

3. EXERCISE OF SPIRITUAL GIFTS

What about the exercise or manifestation of certain spiritual gifts like healing, prophecy, word of knowledge, word of wisdom, miracles, etc.? The Corinthian Church was the most Gifted Church in the New Testament as testified by Paul. They did not lack any Gift, yet, they were the most carnal Church. No Church in the New Testament exhibited as much carnality as they did – church divisions and factions, fornication, lawsuits among brethren, misuse of Spiritual Gifts and improper behaviour at the Lord's Table, to mention a few (1 Corinthians 3).

Have you noticed the new wave of the manifestation of the Gifts of the Spirit in operation in the Body of Christ, particularly the Gift of Prophecy? Almost everywhere you turn, you meet a Prophet or someone who exercises the Gift of Prophecy. However, I have come across a few 'prophets' that are nothing but diviners.

Jesus shows us that the exercise of Spiritual Gifts is no guarantee for divine approval, for many who perform great feats in the Name of the Lord will still be refused or rejected:

"Not every one that saith unto me, Lord, Lord, shall enter into the kingdom of heaven; but he that doeth the will of my Father which is in heaven. Many will say to me in that day, Lord, Lord, have we not prophesied in thy name? and in thy name have cast out devils? and in thy name done many wonderful works? And then will I profess unto them, I never knew you: depart from me, ye that work iniquity."

– Matthew 7:21-23 (KJV).

4. WORKING IN THE MINISTRY

Most people will often consider working in a Ministry or Church environment a sure sign of Spiritual Maturity. However, there are many people that we have all met, including Pastors and full-time

Christian workers, who didn't demonstrate or exhibit any sign of Spiritual Maturity. In fact, we wondered whether they ever met the Lord. Is it possible to be 'working' for God and yet not walking with Him?

SIGNS OF SPIRITUAL MATURITY

Now that we have identified some things that do not constitute Spiritual Maturity, let's examine a few signs or pointers to the fact that a Christian is maturing in Christ:

1. PLACES GREAT VALUE ON ETERNAL THINGS

One of the things that sets a carnal Believer apart from a matured one is that the matured Saint places a great premium on eternal things. This person measures or views everything – their time, talents, treasures, relationships, etc. from an eternal perspective.

Moses exhibited this spiritual trait, for it was written of him that

"By faith Moses, when he was come to years, refused to be called the son of Pharaoh's daughter; Choosing rather to suffer affliction with the people of God, than to enjoy the pleasures of sin for a season; Esteeming the reproach of Christ greater riches than the treasures in Egypt: for he had respect unto the recompence of the reward."
– Hebrews 11:24-26 (KJV).

On the contrary, Esau was called a profane person, because he placed temporal pleasures above Spiritual realities.

"Lest there be *any fornicator, or profane person, as Esau, who for one morsel of meat sold his birthright."*

– Hebrews 12:16 (KJV).

2.   MANIFESTING THE FRUIT OF THE SPIRIT

One of the key signs that a Believer is growing in the things of the Spirit is the manifestation of the Fruits of the Spirit, as highlighted in Galatians 5:22-23. These nine fruits are produced in the life of Saints, as they allow the Spirit to direct and influence their lives, that they destroy sin's power, especially the acts of the sinful nature, and walk in fellowship with God.

3.   THE EXCHANGED LIFE

Another sign of Spiritual Maturity is when a Believer is living the exchanged or crucified life. This is when we allow the indwelling nature of Christ to live out in us:

"I am crucified with Christ: nevertheless I live; yet not I, but Christ liveth in me: and the life which I now live in the flesh I live by the faith of the Son of God, who loved me, and gave himself for me."

- Galatians 2:20 (KJV).

The big question is – are you still living on your own terms or are you allowing Christ to live through you?

4. HUNGER FOR SPIRITUAL THINGS

No doubt, a hunger for spiritual things is an indication that you are progressing or maturing in Christ. I have met so many people who claim to be Christians, but have little or no appetite for Spiritual things like fellowship, soul–winning, prayer, Bible reading, Studying and meditation, to mention these few. A hunger for Spiritual things is a sure sign of Spiritual Maturity.

5. GIVING

Spiritual people always take delight in Giving. Be it their time, talents, or treasures. This is not always the case for carnal Believers, who are mostly self-centred, and would sometimes give if they expect a return or favours.

6. SERVANTHOOD AND HUMILITY

One of the distinguishing marks of a growing Believer or Leader is their desire to be a Servant. All Spiritual giants over the centuries, including our Saviour, Jesus Christ, have been great servants (Philippians 2:5-11). Elisha, who inherited a double portion of Elijah's spirit, was described or introduced as one that "poured water" on the hands of Elijah.

That is, he was a servant. Paul always introduced himself as a bond slave – a mark of great humility from an Apostle who was Primus - inter - pares.

CHAPTER 6
CONSEQUENCES OF SPIRITUAL STAGNATION

There are only a few things that are more abhorring, frustrating and heart-breaking than dealing with Christians who just refuse to grow.

Any parent who has dealt with stagnation in the life of a child's education, for example, will tell you the pain, heartbreak and often shame that they have to endure. Just as there are grave consequences when a child's education is retarded, so also are there attendant problems when Christians refuse to grow.

The following are some of the consequences of spiritual retardation or stagnation:

1. CHRISTIAN WITNESSING IS HINDERED
    As Christians, we are called to be the Light of the world. Jesus declared that we are to be His Witnesses

after we have received the Holy Spirit (Acts 1:8). This means, we are not just to preach with words, but our lives should be Epistles seen and read by men. When Christians refuse to mature into the Image of Christ, it drives unbelievers away from Christ. How many souls leave the Church because of the carnal and ungodly behaviour of a "Christian" brother or sister? Some of you must have heard an unbelieving person remark "...and you call yourself a Christian?" or "is this what your Bible teaches?"

Do you know the Bible actually teaches that a Christian woman can win her unsaved husband over without preaching to him but by her conduct or behaviour?

"Likewise, ye wives, be *in subjection to your own husbands; that, if any obey not the word, they also may without the word be won by the conversation of the wives."*

– 1 Peter 3:1 (KJV).

I am totally convinced that we will witness more people flocking into the Kingdom if more Christians will mature into Christ's Image and demonstrate the true virtues of the Kingdom.

2. HAMPERS THE PROGRESS OF THE WORK OF THE KINGDOM

Not only does spiritual stagnation affect

Christian witnessing in the unbelieving world, it also slows down, sets back and destroys the work of the Kingdom. Have you ever considered the negative impact carnal behaviours and attitudes have on Kingdom work? What happens when a supposed Christian husband habitually cheats on his wife? What about Christian wives who will never submit but rather manipulate their husbands?

So many ministerial assignments have been cut short or aborted because one partner just refused to grow! How many children from Christian homes have been pushed into drugs, gangs, fraud, and immoral lifestyles because of the negative impact of one or both of their parents who were meant to be Godly examples? What happens to the cause of Christ, when a Believer wants to always have their way? What about modern day Christianity where most Believers are just unwilling to sacrifice anything, rather, they simply want to serve God out of convenience? No doubt, spiritual stagnation is the root of all evil in the Church today!

3. DISQUALIFICATION FROM REIGNING WITH CHRIST

It is one thing for a Believer to make it to heaven, and yet another for them to reign with Christ in the Millennial Kingdom. Many Believers don't see a correlation between the life that we live now and the one to come. Life on earth now, for a Believer, is a training ground for the life to come. Did you know that rulership in the Millennial Kingdom is only for those who have a Christ-like character? Authority, rulership and responsibilities will be awarded to Believers in the Millennial Kingdom.

Let's check a few scriptures to substantiate the viewpoint:

"Then shall the kingdom of heaven be likened unto ten virgins, which took their lamps, and went forth to meet the bridegroom. And five of them were wise, and five were foolish. They that were foolish took their lamps, and took no oil with them: But the wise took oil in their vessels with their lamps. While the bridegroom tarried, they all slumbered and slept. And at midnight there was a cry made, Behold, the bridegroom cometh; go ye out to meet him. Then all those virgins arose, and trimmed their lamps. And the foolish said unto the wise, Give us of your oil; for our lamps are gone out. But the wise answered, saying, Not so; lest there be not enough for us and you: but go ye rather to them that sell, and buy for yourselves. And while they went to buy, the bridegroom came; and they that were ready went in with him to the marriage: and the door was shut. Afterward came also the other virgins, saying, Lord, Lord, open to us. But he answered and said, Verily I say unto you, I know you not. Watch therefore, for

ye know neither the day nor the hour wherein the Son of man cometh."

– **Matthew 25:1-13 (KJV).**

This parable is known as the parable of the foolish and wise virgins. This parable is really dealing with how some Christians will be disqualified from the Millennial Kingdom. Notice the following – all the ten individuals were virgins. That is, they were genuinely born again. Furthermore, they also all had their lamps – which signifies the Word of God and oil – representing the Holy Spirit.

However, what distinguished the foolish from the wise virgins was that they didn't have extra oil. These represent Believers, who can't go the extra mile in their Relationship with Christ. Commitment here is the key! There are many today who can't sacrifice worldly and passing pleasures to deepen their Relationship with the Holy Spirit. They are simple fair-weather Christians. As Believers, there is the need for perseverance in the Faith, in view of the delay in Christ's coming.

Again, Paul writes:

"Know ye not that they which run in a race run all, but one receiveth the prize? So run, that ye may obtain. And every man that striveth for the mastery is temperate in all things. Now they do it to obtain a corruptible crown; but we an incorruptible. I

therefore so run, not as uncertainly; so fight I, not as one that beateth the air: But I keep under my body, and bring it into subjection: lest that by any means, when I have preached to others, I myself should be a castaway."
– **1 Corinthians 9:24-27 (KJV).**

In this passage, Paul was using the Isthmian League, and later, the Olympic Games and what obtains there, to teach his readers a lesson about running for eternal rewards. So, what lessons can we learn from this passage? First, it is not everyone that runs in a race who receives a prize or is crowned. We can run the Christian race and still be disqualified if we don't run according to the rules. Every Christian must run to obtain the prize. This entails passion, purpose, and strict training.

Discipline is the key to obtaining the crown. In Paul's day, just as today, athletes have to exercise strict discipline with regards to diets, sleep and training. In verse twenty-seven, Paul raises an important issue – the exercise of Spiritual Gifts, which are by no means a guarantee of acceptance with God. One could still be a castaway or disqualified.

How often do we hear today on our pulpits that one can be a Christian, yet they could be disqualified from reigning with Christ in the Millennial Kingdom because they have not lived according to the rules of the Kingdom?

THE BRITISH ROYAL FAMILY

I will love to use the example of the British royal family to drive home my point. It is one thing to be born into the royal family – this is the easy bit because it isn't by choice, but by Grace. Prince Charles, the heir apparent, wasn't born into the royal family by choice, it was by Grace. However, what is more difficult is to be conformed to what it means to be a member of the royal family, particularly an heir apparent. While British subjects don't bother much with all the rules, regulations, values, etiquettes and protocol, royal family members, on the other hand, have to be trained, schooled and groomed specially to live out and conform to the expectations of being royal. To reign with Christ, we will also have to undergo strict or disciplined lifestyles on earth.

CHAPTER 7

WHY THE DOMA GIFTS?

The DOMA Gifts have been called by different names or appellations, including the five and four-fold Gifts. Others have called it the Ministry or Ascension Gifts.

It has often been said that when purpose is lost, abuse is inevitable. The Ministry or Ascension Gifts, in my estimation, are one of the most misunderstood and abused Gifts in the Church today. How do I know that these Gifts are misunderstood by a large percentage of the members of the Body of Christ? My answer is simple – by people's expectations. If you look at what the Church expects from their leaders, you might be shocked. Some Believers have made gods out of their Pastors, and many don't even understand the biblical roles of the Ascension Gifts.

Paul, in his Epistle to the Ephesians, indicates some of the foremost purposes of which Christ gives gifted Leaders to the Church.

> *"And he gave some, apostles; and some, prophets; and some, evangelists; and some, pastors and teachers; For the perfecting of the saints, for the work of the ministry, for the edifying of the body of Christ: Till we all come in the unity of the faith, and of the knowledge of the Son of God, unto a perfect man, unto the measure of the stature of the fulness of Christ."*
> **– Ephesians 4:11-13 (KJV).**

The DOMA gifts are given to the Church to train, equip, and prepare the whole Body to do the work of the Ministry. The model whereby the 'professional' Minister does most of the Ministry work, and the Saints simply watch or observe, is totally foreign to the New Testament. Also, as a result of the Ministry or work of the Church Leaders, the Believers were to become perfect men, to the measure of the stature of the fullness of Christ.

Is this part of your goal as a Christian Leader? Are your Ministry teachings structured towards this goal? Do we preach or teach with a view of making the Believers conformed to the Image of their Saviour? To some Ministers, the answer is in the negative. Many Servants of God simply focus on messages that will gratify the carnal, selfish, and self-centred cravings of the Believers. Many Pastors never preach or focus on the person of Christ. Too often, we limit our messages to the principles of the Kingdom. This is why a high percentage of Believers know little or nothing about Christ. Our Church meetings, conferences and seminars are nothing more than a shopping exercise, where we go and present all our needs and greed to a Father Christmas called God.

May I submit to you today that if we are to raise Believers who will be conformed to Christ's Image, we might have to alter our teachings, programmes and thrust.

CHAPTER 8

WHAT ON EARTH ARE WE FEEDING THE CHURCH?

A common saying, which I wholeheartedly believe is, "you are what you eat."

One of the new emphases in modern medicine is the place or importance of a good diet in a person's well-being. This means that if one is to live a healthy life, you must make sure that you not only eat a balanced diet, but there are certain foods that you must avoid. You cannot completely be eating junk food - foods with bad fat, white sugar and the like, and expect to live a healthy life.

The place of Pastors and Spiritual Leaders in the overall spiritual growth or development of the average Believer cannot be over emphasised. We are responsible for their spiritual oversight; we largely dictate what their spiritual diet looks like. First, the Pastor – teacher, feeds his flock regularly. Again, he or she is also in charge of the invited guests who speak into the lives of their flock.

This fact underlines the reason why Jesus charged Peter, one of the pillars of the early Church, to take the issue of the spiritual nourishment of his flock seriously. Thrice, Jesus repeated Himself:

> *"So when they had dined, Jesus saith to Simon Peter, Simon, son of Jonas, lovest thou me more than these? He saith unto him, Yea, Lord; thou knowest that I love thee. He saith unto him, Feed my lambs. He saith to him again the second time, Simon, son of Jonas, lovest thou me? He saith unto him, Yea, Lord; thou knowest that I love thee. He saith unto him, Feed my sheep. He saith unto him the third time, Simon, son of Jonas, lovest thou me? Peter was grieved because he said unto him the third time, Lovest thou me? And he said unto him, Lord, thou knowest all things; thou knowest that I love thee. Jesus saith unto him, Feed my sheep."*
> **– John 21:15-17 (KJV).**

Again Paul, the erudite scholar from Tarsus, in his valedictory speech to the Ephesian elders, underlines the importance he attached to feeding God's Church with the right diet:

"And from Miletus he sent to Ephesus, and called the elders of the church. And when they were come to him, he said unto them, Ye know, from the first day that I came into Asia, after what manner I have been with you at all seasons, Serving the Lord with all humility of mind, and with many tears, and temptations, which befell me by the lying in wait of the Jews: And how I kept back nothing that was profitable unto you, but have shewed you, and have taught you publickly, and from house to house, Testifying both to the Jews, and also to the Greeks, repentance toward God, and faith toward our Lord Jesus Christ."

– Acts 20:17-21 (KJV).

Notice with me that Paul preached whatever he believed was needful or useful for the salvation and spiritual nourishment of his hearers.

As Ministers of the Gospel, we are to preach the undiluted, uncompromising Word of God. We are to teach the total counsel of God; we are not just to preach what is popular or acceptable. Preachers and Teachers of the Word of God, like any responsible parent, must serve a balanced spiritual diet.

"For I have not shunned to declare unto you all the counsel of God."

– Acts 20:27 (KJV).

As Ministers of the Gospel, the Spiritual menu that we serve God's heritage must contain at least four important ingredients –
- Doctrine
- Reproof
- Correction
- Instruction in Righteousness.

"All scripture is given by inspiration of God, and is profitable for doctrine, for reproof, for correction, for instruction in righteousness:"
— **2 Timothy 3:16 (KJV).**

WHAT DOES YOUR TEACHING PROGRAM LOOK LIKE?

Any serious Pastor or Apostolic Leader must take seriously the teaching Ministry of his Church. Just as good food is crucial to the well-being of any family, so also is a well-balanced, Christ-centred teaching programme critical to the spiritual well-being of the flock. There must be a deliberate attempt to teach the Church. It must be well structured, and the content vetted by the Senior Pastor or an Elder, or even a committee made up of spiritually sound persons.

From the moment an individual becomes a Christian or joins the Church, there must be a series of classes, teachings, discipleship and mentoring programmes, aimed at growing the individual into the Image of Christ. Unfortunately, many Pastors don't pay attention to their teaching ministry. A large percentage of Churches and denominations don't have any basic qualifications prescribed for those who lead congregations. This, in turn, affects the quality of the teaching programmes in several Churches or Ministries.

I must commend a number of the older denominations, who have a solid teaching Ministry. I have always argued that Ministries that run solid, Bible-based and Christ-centred, teaching programmes are more likely to produce Believers who honour Christ in their societies.

Over the years, I have run a number of classes – they include foundation classes, discipleship classes, maturity and Ministry classes, etc. This is different from Ministry and mentoring opportunities.

CHAPTER 9

SPIRITUAL MATURITY AND ADVERSITY

"Though he were a Son, yet learned he obedience by the things which he suffered."
— **Hebrews 5:8 (KJV).**

The Bible makes it abundantly clear that Christians are to expect suffering and adversities if they are going to live their lives in line with the Scriptures and pleasing to God. This is why we are not to think it strange when we go through diverse trials. Furthermore, it seems that God allows His children to go through sufferings, afflictions or adversities in order to mature them. No doubt in God's training, suffering, adversities and afflictions are part of the curriculum.

JOSEPH

Joseph is a classic example of maturing through adversity. After God had revealed twice to Joseph, his destiny in life, the natural expectation was that this dream would be fulfilled on a platter of gold. Joseph would have thought that his march into the palace would definitely be a smooth one. He was mistaken! He had to travel through the road of sufferings, afflictions and adversities.

First, his brothers hated him and could not speak peacefully to him, then he was thrown into a pit. Like Jesus, he was sold for money to the Ishmaelite traders and ended up as a slave in the house of Potiphar. He suffered slander for not committing sexual immorality with his master's wife. For this, he was thrown into prison. It was while he was serving his prison sentence that God's Prophetic Word was fulfilled in his life. If we reflect upon his life, particularly his foundation years, one might ask – why the suffering and affliction? What was the purpose of his adversities? I believe it was meant to mature him; to prepare him for reigning. God was trying to build his character. The only reason Joseph would not retaliate and punish his brothers for all the evil he suffered in their hands was because God had processed in him Christ-like character.

God uses afflictions and sufferings to develop character in His children. This is why James urges Believers to endure their trials joyfully.

> *"My brethren, count it all joy when ye fall into divers temptations; Knowing this, that the trying of your faith worketh patience."*
> **– James 1:2-3 (KJV).**

I will share a personal opinion and I know that some people will disagree with me, but I'm also sure that many will agree with my observation. Churches and Christians that have experienced great suffering and affliction are usually more spiritual than those who have had a smooth sailing in life. They usually have a spiritual depth of the things of God that is foreign to many. Consider the Faith of Believers in China, North Korea, and many Muslim countries. Their faith, prayer focus, sacrifice, and dedication is something that we westerners cannot comprehend.

Jesus, the Son of God – perfect in nature and character, had to learn obedience through what He suffered.

CHAPTER 10
ISRAEL SPEAKS TO US TODAY!

For Believers who are still in doubt about the importance of how they live here and now, Paul, the Apostle evokes some lessons from history by pointing us to Israel:

> *"Moreover, brethren, I would not that ye should be ignorant, how that all our fathers were under the cloud, and all passed through the sea; And were all baptized unto Moses in the cloud and in the sea; And did all eat the same spiritual meat; And did all drink the same spiritual drink: for they drank of that spiritual Rock that followed them: and that Rock was Christ. But with many of them God was not well pleased: for they were overthrown in the wilderness. Now these things were our examples, to the intent we should not lust after evil things, as they also lusted. Neither*

be ye idolaters, as were some of them; as it is written, The people sat down to eat and drink, and rose up to play. Neither let us commit fornication, as some of them committed, and fell in one day three and twenty thousand. Neither let us tempt Christ, as some of them also tempted, and were destroyed of serpents. Neither murmur ye, as some of them also murmured, and were destroyed of the destroyer. Now all these things happened unto them for ensamples: and they are written for our admonition, upon whom the ends of the world are come. Wherefore let him that thinketh he standeth take heed lest he fall."
— **1 Corinthians 10:1-12 (KJV).**

From verses one to four, Paul narrates the various spiritual experiences that Israel enjoyed, and yet, what was their end? Destruction! Only Joshua and Caleb, of the original generation that left Egypt, made it to the Promised Land. Verses six to ten highlight their shortcomings while the whole thrust of the passage lies in verses six and eleven. Here, it is revealed that these experiences are meant to be examples for all of us to learn from and be guided. Enjoying certain spiritual blessings do not preclude us from being disqualified in the end.

Finally, the place of the wilderness experience in the life of every Believer is key. Israel had to pass through the wilderness after they left Egypt. In fact, it was God that led them through the way of the wilderness, even though there was a shorter journey.

> *"And it came to pass, when Pharaoh had let the people go, that God led them not through the way of the land of the Philistines, although that was near; for God said, Lest peradventure the people repent when they see war, and they return to Egypt: But God led the people about, through the way of the wilderness of the Red sea: and the children of Israel went up harnessed out of the land of Egypt."*
> **– Exodus 13:17-18 (KJV).**

What was the purpose of the wilderness experience? It was meant to be a place of testing, like Christ. The wilderness was meant to be a place of training and cleansing, to prepare them for the land of promise. Even though Israel had come out of Egypt, Egypt, with its values and character, had not left them. The experience in the wilderness was meant to refine and build character in God's Redeemed People.

The same principle applies today. After the new birth, God will often allow His children to pass through the wilderness experience in order to develop Christ-like character and total dependence on Him. Too many Believers are ignorant of the purpose of their wilderness season. Quite often, we can resist the dealings of God, and at other times, they think it is the workings of Satan. Afflictions, trials and tests are part of God's curriculum in preparing us for the life-after. Just as Israel had to pass through the wilderness to be tested, so also did the Son of God have to go through the wilderness to be tested.

While Israel failed woefully, Jesus Christ passed His test. What God did for His Son, the First Son among many brethren, He will also do for us. Any lesson from Israel's wilderness experience for us today? I believe a lot!

CHAPTER 11
LIKE FATHER, LIKE SON

"... because as he is, so are we in this world."
– 1 John 4:17b (KJV).

When you hear someone say – "Like father like son", what do they mean? What are they trying to convey? They are simply saying that you possess certain characteristics of your father. It indicates that you are a true reflection of who he is, and what he stands for. It is the same when they say – "he is a chip off the old block!"

It is expected that children will take certain traits, features and characteristics of their parents. For this not to happen, their paternity will be called to question.

I have often heard people remark as a compliment that 'this child behaves like you, or that one walks like you and the other, possesses your heart'. For my children not to take any one of my traits will be really disturbing.

The apple, they say, doesn't fall far from the tree! Jesus, as we know, was a true reflection of the Father. He came to reveal to us who the Father or God is. This was what He was saying when He declared to Phillip:

> *"Jesus saith unto him, Have I been so long time with you, and yet hast thou not known me, Philip? he that hath seen me hath seen the Father; and how sayest thou then, Shew us the Father?"*
> **– John 14:9 (KJV).**

> *"Who is the image of the invisible God, the firstborn of every creature."*
> **-Colossians 1:15 (KJV).**

> *"... lest the light of the glorious gospel of Christ, who is the image of God, should shine unto them."*
> **– 2 Corinthians 4:4b (KJV).**

The question before us as Christians is how well do we look like Jesus? Do we reflect his image and character? The unfortunate thing is that a high percentage of Christians don't look like, or act like Jesus. This is very sad! As Believers and followers of Christ, we are to talk, walk and behave like Him. After all, we are Christians – 'Little Christs'.

We must always remember that the word 'Christian' was given to followers of Christ – not by regenerate people, but the unbelieving world, who saw in the early Believers in Antioch Christ-likeness.

The fundamental question we must always ask ourselves is – am I living like Christ? Does my lifestyle, character, Christian walk, reflect Christ?

SPECIAL INVITATION

I am totally convinced that this book did not come into your hands by sheer accident – it was orchestrated by God!

If you have never at any point in time opened up your heart to receive Jesus and accept Him as your Lord and Personal Saviour – you can do so right now!

Why not say this short prayer?

Dear Jesus! Thank you for dying on the Cross for me.
I believe you died and God raised you up on the third day for my salvation. I accept you today as my Lord and Personal Saviour.
Thank you for saving me! Amen!

OTHER TITLES FROM THE SAME AUTHOR

If this book has touched you, why not place an order for other books!

1. *Great Britain Has Fallen*
2. *Awake Great Britain*
3. *Awake Canada*
4. *Pastoral Abuse*
5. *The Call of God*
6. *The Parable of the Pound*
7. *Dreams: From Conception to Reality*
8. *Fulfilling Your Destiny*
9. *Occupying Vacant Position*
10. *The Wilderness Experience*
11. *Overcoming the Enemy Within*
12. *Great Men and Women who made Great Britain Great*

13. *Benefits of Affliction*
14. *You Can Plead your Case*
15. *The 401 Prophet*
16. *Barrenness; Its Curses and Cures*
17. *Finishing Your Assignment In Life*

CONTACT DETAILS

World Harvest Christian Centre
Great Commission House
25-27 Ruby Street
off Old Kent Road
London SE15 1LL
Tel: + 44 (020) 7358 8080

World Harvest Christian Centre
Enmore Road
South Norwood
London SE25 5NQ
Tel: + 44 (020) 86545649

Email: admin@worldharvest.org.uk
website: www.worldharvest.org.uk
Facebook: World Harvest Christian Centre, London
Twitter: @whcc_london, @PastorWale_